Gift of the
Hackbarth Foundation
2015

MODERN
SPIES

BY SEAN STEWART PRICE

Consultant:
Jan Goldman, EdD
Founding Board Member
International Intelligence Ethics Association
Washington, D.C.

CAPSTONE PRESS
a capstone imprint

Velocity Books are published by Capstone Press,
1710 Roe Crest Drive, North Mankato, Minnesota 56003
www.capstonepub.com

Library of Congress Cataloging-in-Publication Data
Price, Sean.
Modern spies / by Sean Stewart Price.
pages cm. — (Velocity. classified)
Includes bibliographical references and index.
Summary: "Describes the dangerous missions of several modern-day spies"—Provided by
publisher.
ISBN 978-1-4765-0123-9 (library binding)
ISBN 978-1-4765-3589-0 (ebook PDF)
1. Spies—Juvenile literature. 2. Intelligence service—Juvenile literature. 3. Espionage—
Juvenile literature. I. Title.
JF1525.I6P76 2014
327.12092'2—dc23   2013009490

Editorial Credits
Mandy Robbins, editor; Veronica Scott, designer; Jennifer Walker, production specialist

Photo Credits
Alamy: Caro, 14-15; AP Images: Nick Ut, 35, Ric Francis, 39, Sayyid Azim, 29, The News &
Observer, 31; Corbis: Dan Joyce, 32, Richard A. Bloom, 27, Sygma/David Samson, 23, 24;
Department of Defense photo, 40; Gamma-Keystone via Getty Images: Keystone-France, 9;
Getty Images: Alex Wong, 20; iStockphotos: The Power of Forever Photography, 12 (jail);
Newscom: ABACAUSA.COM/Julien Fouchet, 41, Getty Images/AFP/Mohammad Rauf,
44, Getty Images/AFP/Paul J. Richards, 17, Pakistan Press International/Babar Shah, 43,
ZUMA Press/Michael Evans, 11, ZUMA Press/Sing Tao Dally, 36; Shutterstock: Aleksandar
Mijatovic, 34, 38-39 (background), chamsitr, 7, Cristi Matei, 12-13, Fabio Berti, 5, Feng Yu, 19,
Iakov Filimonov, 18, justasc, 8-9, Kheng Guan Toh, 4 (background), 28,31, 33 (background),
Lightspring, 6, Mopic, cover (numbers), ostill, 4 (man), Richard Laschon, 16, SCOTTCHAN,
10, SMA Studio, cover (man), 45, Tatiana Popova, 21, 26 (handcuffs), Undergroundarts.
co.uk, 20, 21 (fingerprints); U.S. Army photo by Staff Sgt. Paul Caron, 30

Artistic Effects
Shutterstock

Direct Quotes
p. 10 from http://www.executedtoday.com/2013/01/23/; p. 15 from Kostin, Sergei,
and Eric Raynaud and Richard V. Allen. Farewell: The Greatest Spy Story of the Twentieth
Century. AmazonCrossing, August 2, 2011. (page 360); p. 16 from http://www.iwp.edu/
events/detail/10th-anniversary-of-the-arrest-of-fbi-agent-robert-hanssen; p. 17 from Wise,
David. Spy: The Inside Story of How the FBI's Robert Hanssen Betrayed America. Random
House Digital, Inc., 2002.; p. 21 from http://www.spy-stories.com/true-spy-stories/
robert-hanssen/; p. 22 from Earley, Pete. Confessions of a Spy: The Real Story of Aldrich Ames.
New York: Penguin Group (USA) Incorporated, 1997. (p. 147); p. 26 from https://www.
cia.gov/news-information/featured-story-archive/ames-mole-hunt-team.html; p. 38 from
http://www.usnews.com/news/articles/2003/11/02/china-doll-was-a-chinese-american-
temptress-really-a-secret-agent.

Printed in the United States of America in Stevens Point, Wisconsin.
042014   008215R

TABLE OF CONTENTS

SPYING IN THE MODERN WORLD

Spies sneak around everywhere. They are in every country and work for every government. These secret agents look and listen for information. They copy top-secret documents. And they risk their lives.

Modern spies work for many reasons and in many conflicts. In recent times, shifting situations in the world have influenced where spies are most often needed.

THE COLD WAR

From 1945 to 1991, there was great tension between the United States and the Soviet Union. The United States favored democracy and **capitalism**. The Soviet Union favored **communism**. Under the communist system, there was little freedom, and all businesses were government-owned.

This period of tension was called the Cold War. Both sides were well-stocked with nuclear weapons. But they were afraid to use them because nuclear weapons can destroy so much so quickly.

Most wars are fought with soldiers. But the Cold War was fought mainly with spies. In 1991 the conflict ended when the Soviet Union collapsed. The country broke up into several smaller countries, the largest of which was Russia. Relations between the United States and Russia are friendlier than they were during the Cold War. But spies still snoop around for both of these former enemies.

capitalism—an economic system that allows people to freely create businesses and own as much property as they can afford

communism—a system in which goods and property are owned by the government and shared in common; communist rulers limit personal freedoms to achieve their goals

THE MIDDLE EAST

The United States has a big interest in the Middle East. Much of the world's oil comes from there. Most people who live in the Middle East are Muslim. They are believers in the religion of Islam. Some Muslims respect the United States. But some think the United States is evil. These **extremists** show their anger by using violence and **terrorism**.

CULTURE CLASH

Why do Muslim extremists see the United States as an enemy? There are many reasons, but here are three important ones:

- The United States is a strong supporter of Israel. Israel is a mostly Jewish country with a long history of fighting with Muslim neighbors.
- Some Muslims believe that their countries should be ruled by strict Islamic laws and customs. The U.S. government promotes more freedom and choice. Muslim extremists see this openness as a threat to their religion.
- The United States has supported many Middle Eastern leaders who oppose an Islamic terrorist organization called al-Qaida.

CHINA

China has the world's largest population. But until the 1980s, it was an extremely poor country. Its communist leaders are eager to see China's economy and military grow strong. They want to see the country become as strong as the United States. For this reason many Chinese spies focus on America, and U.S. spies do the same with China.

extremist—a person whose views or actions are far beyond the norm

terrorism—the use of violence and destructive acts to create fear and advance a strong set of beliefs that may be political or religious

CODENAME FAREWELL

In 1982 a giant explosion rocked Siberia in the eastern Soviet Union. A brand-new pipeline carrying natural gas exploded. No one was hurt in the event. But the explosion rocked the Soviet government. It forced officials there to question all the country's new inventions.

Why? Because a spy in Moscow had a big hand in the explosion. His code name was "Farewell."

"Farewell's" real name was Vladimir Vetrov. He worked for the **KGB**, the chief Soviet spy agency. In the early 1980s, Vetrov became tired of the Soviet Union's communist system. He was especially disgusted with the KGB. Vetrov had seen the KGB arrest people for simply complaining about the Soviet government. He had seen public money spent on expensive parties and gifts for politicians and government officials.

KGB—Russian initials for the Soviet Union's Committee for State Security

Vetrov's work in the KGB focused on stealing science and business secrets from other countries. Soviet scientists made few breakthroughs themselves. They relied on stolen information from other countries. It allowed them to steal designs for the computers, machines, and weapons used by the United States.

construction workers building the Siberian pipeline

FACT:
When the Soviet Union fell in 1991, the KGB was replaced by the Federal Security Service (FSS).

In 1980 Vetrov decided to become a **double agent**. He contacted a French spy agency. He offered to hand over information about how the KGB was stealing technology. Between the spring of 1981 and early 1982, Vetrov gave the French almost 4,000 secret papers. They included the complete list of 250 Soviet spies stealing technology in other countries.

The French gave Vetrov the code name "Farewell." French President François Mitterrand gave Farewell's information to U.S. President Ronald Reagan in a file called the Farewell Dossier.

Farewell's information showed Americans just how much technology the Soviets were stealing. So the Central Intelligence Agency (CIA) decided to plant bogus technology. Bad computer chips made it into Soviet military equipment. Flawed machines ran in Soviet factories. Even the Soviet space shuttle was based on a rejected U.S. design.

"OUR SCIENCE WAS SUPPORTING THEIR NATIONAL DEFENSE."
— GUS W. WEISS, CIA OFFICIAL

double agent—a spy who works for one country's spy agency but is really loyal to another

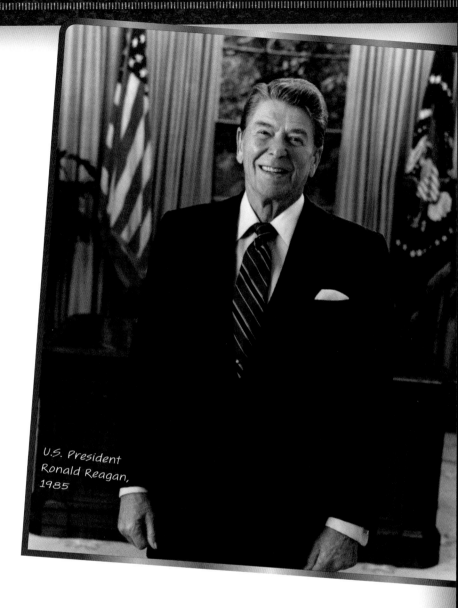

U.S. President
Ronald Reagan,
1985

The Soviets wanted a computer control system for their
new gas pipeline in Siberia. It was an important pipeline
that would bring in billions of dollars to the economy.
It would also help the Soviets control European gas
production. The CIA leaked a system to the Soviets through
a Canadian company. It looked like it would work when
tested. But when used for real, it would explode.

The CIA's plan worked. When the Soviets started using the pipeline, the software caused the explosion in Siberia. But by that point, Vetrov was in serious trouble. The stress of being a spy weighed on him. In February 1982, he was arrested and jailed for injuring a woman and killing a man during a violent outburst. When questioned by the police, Vetrov let it slip that he had also spied against his country. He was executed as a traitor in 1983.

A DANGEROUS ERROR

The U.S. effort to hurt Soviet computers almost backfired. A Soviet space satellite kept track of U.S. nuclear missiles. In June 1983 the satellite suddenly began making wild mistakes because its flawed chips came from the United States. The satellite reported that the Americans were firing their missiles at the Soviet Union. This could have set off a nuclear war. But the Soviets quickly saw that the satellite was wrong.

Vetrov had set important changes in motion. The Soviets fell further and further behind the United States in creating new military technology. The Americans began building supercomputers that could control large nuclear missile systems. But the Soviets could not catch up by stealing secrets from other countries.

At the same time, the United States announced that they were making more complicated weapons. These weapons included airplanes that could not be spotted by radar. The United States also announced plans to create space-based weapons. By 1987 Soviet leaders admitted that they were hopelessly behind the United States.

THE LAST WORD

Although Vetrov was executed, in some ways he had the last word. One of his last acts was to write a paper titled *Confessions of a Traitor*. The long document was an attack on the Soviet system of government. It was widely read within the KGB. Many people agreed with his arguments. Meanwhile, the information Vetrov gave France destroyed the KGB's program for stealing technology.

Vetrov's spying and writing badly hurt the Soviet government. But it also helped change the Soviet system. Because the Soviets could not compete, they began to make reforms. Some of these reforms gave ordinary people more freedom. A KGB official later said that Vetrov "went to his death with only one regret — that he could not have done more damage to the KGB in his service for France."

The biggest symbol of the fall of the Soviet Union occurred when the Berlin Wall came down on November 11, 1989.

A DOUBLE LIFE IN THE FBI

On February 18, 2001, Robert Hanssen walked into a park near his house in Virginia, just outside of Washington, D.C. When he came to a small footbridge, the longtime Federal Bureau of Investigation (FBI) agent stopped and looked around. Seeing no one, he slipped a small package under the bridge. Then he strolled casually back to his car.

Hanssen was reaching for his keys when two vans appeared out of nowhere. Fellow FBI officers jumped out and rushed up to Hanssen, pointing guns at him. "You're under arrest!" they yelled. "Put your hands in the air!" Stunned, Hanssen was handcuffed before he could obey.

On his way to jail, the agents showed Hanssen the evidence they had that he was a **mole**. They played a tape of him talking to a Russian officer about spying for the former Soviet Union. They showed him letters that he had written to the Russians about his spying. They showed him photos of the dead drops. These were places where he left secret documents unattended for his Russian handlers to find, as he did in the park.

ROBERT HANSSEN

TOP SECRET

16

Hanssen had been spying since 1979. He provided the Soviets and Russians with valuable information about U.S. spies in those countries off and on for 22 years. Hanssen had access to all the FBI's information about the Soviets and Russians. "He knew all the secrets," one former co-worker said.

mole—a spy who works within the government of one country in order to supply secret information to another country

Over his career as a spy, Hanssen was paid more than $600,000 by the Soviets and Russians. But money may not have been his primary motivation. Since childhood, Hanssen had loved the idea of being a famous spy. But at the FBI, he merely studied the information supplied by spies. He knew he would always remain stuck behind a desk there. Hanssen thought becoming a double agent was his way to become a famous spy.

Hanssen proved valuable to the Soviets. His information led to the death and capture of several U.S. spies working against the Soviet Union. It also crippled countless FBI operations aimed at catching Soviet and Russian spies.

THE PERFECT COVER

Few spies had a better cover than Hanssen. He was a devoted family man with six children. He was also an outspoken Roman Catholic. Hanssen even belonged to a conservative group called "Opus Dei." That Catholic organization campaigned against the Soviet Union and its communist beliefs. Few suspected such a committed anti-communist would spy for a communist country.

The FBI had several warning signs that Hanssen was a traitor. One of them came from his own brother-in-law, who was also an FBI agent. He had heard that Hanssen had a large pile of cash—a sign he was doing something illegal.

In the early 1990s, Hanssen **hacked** into a fellow employee's computer. When caught, Hanssen said he only wanted to show that the FBI's computer security needed improvement.

hack—to get into a computer system illegally

By the late 1990s, FBI officials knew there was a mole in the department, but they could not discover who it was. A break came in September 2000, when a Russian double agent gave the FBI files that the mole had delivered to the KGB. The file included a plastic bag. Hanssen's fingerprints were on the bag.

The FBI quietly began watching Hanssen. He was videotaped taking secret documents from the FBI office. The FBI **bugged** his home, office, and car. FBI agents also bought a house across the street from Hanssen's home. That made watching him easier.

Hanssen's home was investigated by the FBI after his arrest.

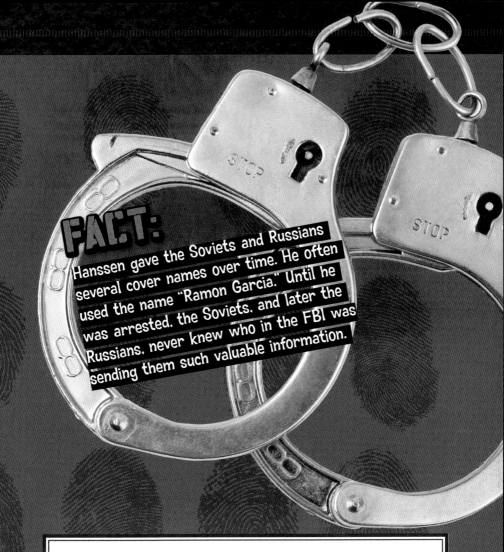

Finally, on February 18, 2001, Hanssen was caught red-handed leaving documents at the park near his house.

"Why did it take you so long?" he said to the men who arrested him.

Some U.S. officials wanted to pursue the death penalty for the man they called the most damaging FBI turncoat in history. Instead, in June 2001, Hanssen cut a deal. He received a life sentence in prison. In return, he had to provide full details of his career as a spy.

bug—to place a hidden microphone

THE MOLE AND THE MOLE HUNTER

Aldrich Ames & Jeanne Vertefeuille

On April 16, 1985, Aldrich Ames walked into the Soviet **embassy** in Washington, D.C. The CIA agent's stated reason for the visit was to meet a Soviet official. He left a present for the Soviets—an envelope with names inside. They were the names of Soviet agents known to the CIA.

Why would Ames, a man who had been with the CIA for 23 years, suddenly spy for the other side? "I did it for the money. Period," he later said. In the note Ames left at the embassy, he told the Soviets that he needed $50,000. He soon had his money.

Ames had planned to send the Soviets information just once. But his first try at spying left him scared. What if a U.S. spy in the Soviet Union could identify him to others in the CIA? Ames decided to fix the problem. He gave the Soviets the names of all 20 CIA agents working in the Soviet government.

embassy—a building in one country where the representatives of another country work; an embassy is treated as a part of the country it represents

Aldrich Ames, 1992

23

The information Ames gave the KGB ruined at least 100 CIA operations in the Soviet Union. U.S. agents in the Soviet Union began disappearing quickly. Most were arrested and some were killed. The CIA realized that something was wrong and set out to discover what it was. Long-time CIA agent Jeanne Vertefeuille (VER-tah-foy) was chosen to lead this effort.

Aldrich Ames on a beach in Mexico with his future wife

It took Vertefeuille's four-person team several years to identify Ames as the culprit. Why? First they had to identify the problem. Had the KGB cracked U.S. codes, allowing the Soviets to read the CIA's mail? Did it have listening devices planted in some CIA offices? Or was there a mole within the CIA? Answering these questions took time. By 1991 Vertefeuille's team was focusing on the mole hunt.

Meanwhile, Ames kept selling secrets to the Soviets. In all, he received $2.5 million for this information. But by 1989, he was already seen as suspicious. One fellow agent pointed out that he seemed to be spending far more than his salary would allow. But at first people in the CIA assumed that this was because his wife's family was wealthy.

FACT:

One of the U.S. agents Ames betrayed, Sergey Fedorenko, had been a friend of his.

Vertefeuille's team investigated Ames' spending habits. Over several years, Ames had made big deposits in his bank account right after meetings with Soviet officials in Washington. Vertefeuille's team soon focused completely on Ames. The FBI was brought in to collect more evidence. Agents found notes about secret meetings in Ames' home trash.

FBI agents arrested Ames in February 1994. They stopped him just before he made a trip to Moscow, Russia. After his arrest, Vertefeuille interviewed Ames about his spying activities. During their talk, Ames told her that he had tried to frame her for his spying. He asked his contacts in Moscow to make it look like she was the mole. But they never did.

At first Vertefeuille was upset that Ames had tried to frame her, but then she started to laugh. "It really was funny," she said, "because he was the one in shackles, not me." Ames was sentenced to life in prison.

Aldrich Ames leaves the courthouse during his 1994 trial.

AL-QAIDA'S SPY

Ali Abdelsoud Mohammed looked just like a tourist. Mohammed wandered around downtown Nairobi, the capital of Kenya, in Africa. He was snapping photos and taking in the sights. Mohammed had two cameras dangling from his neck. And he seemed like a warm, friendly man. People opened up to him easily.

But this 1993 trip was no harmless vacation. Mohammed was picking targets for a terrorist bombing. He was part of the Muslim terrorist group al-Qaida. The group's leader, Osama bin Laden, believed the United States was an enemy of Islam. He wanted to bomb buildings in Nairobi with ties to America.

Mohammed staked out several possible targets. But he decided the U.S. embassy in Nairobi was the best. He found that there was little security. The building was near the street. A truck bomb could just pull up along side it and blow up.

Five years later, on August 7, 1998, that's exactly what happened. A truck bomb rocked the U.S. embassy in Nairobi. Minutes later a similar bomb blew up outside the U.S. embassy in Tanzania, another African country. In all, 213 people were killed and about 4,500 were wounded.

The truck bomb that exploded outside the U.S. embassy in Nairobi on August 7, 1998, caused major destruction.

Not long after the bombings, U.S. authorities began to realize that Mohammed might be a spy. What they found out about him could have come right out of a spy movie.

Mohammed was born in Egypt. He served in the Egyptian Army but was kicked out in 1984 for being a Muslim extremist. A fellow extremist asked Mohammed to join a U.S. intelligence agency. His mission would be to spy on the Americans.

Mohammed was a good candidate for spy work. Besides his native Arabic, he spoke English, French, and Hebrew. During the 1980s, Mohammed married an American woman. Under a special program, he was also allowed to join the U.S. Army. In part because of his military background, he was posted at Fort Bragg in North Carolina. This is where some of America's elite special forces are trained.

AIRBORNE

WELCOME TO

FORT BRAGG

HOME OF THE AIRBORNE

Ali Abdelsoud
Mohammed

In the Army, Mohammed was known as an expert on Muslim culture. He trained and lectured U.S. soldiers about life and politics in the Middle East. He even produced videos about Islam for his fellow soldiers. His superiors described him as being an excellent soldier who did his job well.

At the same time, Mohammed spied against the United States and became closer to al-Qaida leaders. He copied secret maps and military training manuals. Mohammed used these documents to write a training manual for al-Qaida. Mohammed also helped train terrorists directly. This training made al-Qaida much better at carrying out attacks.

Al-Qaida terrorists attacked the World
Trade Center towers on September 11, 2001.

By the early 1990s, Mohammed was also helping the FBI. He was the first person to give the FBI details about al-Qaida. Mohammed continued living a double life. He took many trips overseas. During these trips he trained Osama bin Laden and other top al-Qaida officials.

In 1993 he made a trip to Nairobi to plan the bombing of the embassy there. But by this point the FBI had begun to suspect that Mohammed was a double agent.

After a long investigation, Mohammed was arrested in 1998. After his arrest, Mohammed became a valuable source of information about al-Qaida. U.S. soldiers have reported that he helped show them how to find al-Qaida leaders in other countries. Like many other things about him, the details of what happened after his arrest remain wrapped in secrecy. Mohammed is currently in the witness protection program. Informants whose lives may be in danger are hidden and protected from harm.

AL-QAIDA ATTACKS

In the 1990s and early 2000s, al-Qaida launched several attacks on the United States. In the 1990s, terrorists attacked U.S. embassies and military targets in other countries. On September 11, 2001, a group of 19 men **hijacked** four U.S. passenger airliners. They crashed two planes into the World Trade Center towers in New York City and one into the Pentagon in Washington, D.C. The passengers on the fourth plane fought the hijackers before the plane crashed into a Pennsylvania field. The attacks that day killed nearly 3,000 people.

hijack—to take illegal control of a vehicle, such as an airplane

BETRAYAL BY THE "PARLOR MAID"

On April 10, 2003, people in Los Angeles were shocked to hear that Katrina Leung had been arrested the day before. She was a well-known businesswoman and a respected leader in the city's Chinese-American community. Leung spent time with millionaires and world leaders. But according to the FBI, she was a spy for the Chinese government.

In 1982, when Leung was in her 20s, she started working for the FBI as a counterintelligence **asset**. That meant part of her job was to get information about the Chinese government and military. The other part of her job was to pass along false information about the United States to Chinese spies. The FBI gave her the code name "Parlor Maid."

FBI Special Agent J.J. Smith recruited Leung to work for the bureau. He also worked as her **handler**. Not long after being recruited, Leung and Smith started secretly dating.

Katrina Leung, 2005

asset—an item or person of value
handler—a person at a spy agency who serves as a contact and mentor for spies

35

Katrina Leung at a
formal event in 2000

Leung seemed to have done her job well for the FBI until about 1990. Then something changed. She later said that the Chinese spy agency, the Ministry for State Security (MSS), threatened her with harm if she didn't work for China.

Leung began tipping off the MSS about the identity of undercover FBI agents. When another FBI agent found out about Leung's actions, he let Smith know. At first, Smith was upset and confronted Leung. She confessed that she gave one piece of information to the MSS. But she persuaded Smith not to turn her in. Smith was afraid that if he turned in Leung, she would reveal his relationship with her. If other FBI agents found out the two were dating, Smith would be fired.

THE PRICE OF SPYING

Leung often held expensive parties for important Chinese officials, both in China and the United States. Over time, the FBI paid $1.2 million to cover these and other expenses. Leung also earned $521,000 for passing along phony information from the FBI to the Chinese.

Instead of turning in Leung, Smith covered for her. He even continued to use her as a spy. But Leung kept spying for China. Smith often took secret documents home in his briefcase. When he wasn't looking, Leung went through the briefcase and copied documents. She would then pass them on to the MSS. Smith even let her look over documents he brought home.

Smith's mishandling of Leung was a disaster for U.S. intelligence. Through Smith, Leung could find out about every FBI and CIA spy operation aimed at China. Meanwhile, the Chinese used Leung to feed phony information to Smith. That information helped shape the policies of at least three U.S. presidents.

In November 2000 a CIA official began to suspect Leung was a double agent. But the government made mistakes in the legal case against her. She ended up with a very light sentence. Leung paid a $10,000 fine and served 200 hours of community service. She also served three years **probation** but no jail time. Today she is a free woman.

"We may never know what we lost," said Larry Wortzel, a U.S. expert on spying in China. "What we will never know is if what we got was fed to us and created in China to mislead us, or was real."

Katrina Leung leaving court with
her lawyer and husband in 2003

probation—when a criminal is allowed to go free under the close
supervision of a probation officer

HUNTING OSAMA BIN LADEN

Around 1:00 a.m. on May 1, 2011, people in Abbottabad, Pakistan, were jolted awake. First, they heard low-flying helicopters. That sound was followed by gunfire, shouting, and an explosion. What was going on?

About 23 U.S. Navy **SEALs** swooped into a large compound in Abbottabad. They were after the world's most wanted terrorist, Osama bin Laden. The SEALs found him in a bedroom and shot him. The mastermind behind the September 11, 2001, terrorist attacks was dead.

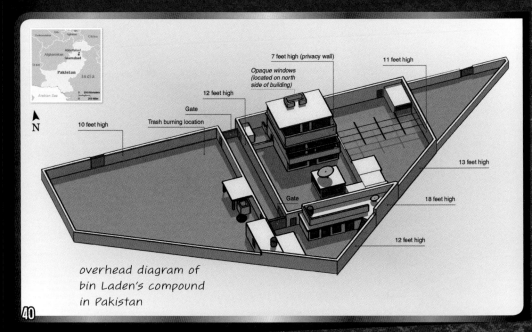

overhead diagram of
bin Laden's compound
in Pakistan

view of bin Laden's compound from outside the fence

The raid on bin Laden's home was daring. But if it hadn't been for months of spy work, U.S. forces would have never found it. In 2010 U.S. officials tracked one of bin Laden's messengers to a large compound in Abbottabad. They wondered if the man was delivering notes to bin Laden there. To find out, they needed the help of spies such as Pakistani doctor Shakeel Afridi.

But finding out if bin Laden lived there was not easy. The compound was surrounded by high walls. It wasn't near many other houses. The people who lived there were very secretive. They even burned their trash. Few neighbors saw the people who lived there, let alone met them. U.S. spy satellites were not much help either. They noticed a tall man who walked around the compound every day, but his identity was uncertain.

SEALs—a special forces group in the U.S. Navy; SEAL stands for "Sea," "Air," and "Land"

One sure way to find out if bin Laden was there was to get a sample of his **DNA**. That's where Afridi came in. He was asked to give **vaccinations** to the people in Abbottabad. The shots would be real. But the needles he used would contain traces of each person's DNA. If one of the needles had bin Laden's DNA, or even the DNA of his children, then he was probably living in the compound.

Afridi's vaccination program didn't work out in the way it was planned. Neither Afridi nor his assistants could persuade the people in the compound to get the shots. But his mission was still a success. While giving shots to other locals, Afridi asked innocent-sounding questions about the people in the compound. He found out some important information. He discovered that neighborhood kids often played ball games near the compound. If the children hit a ball over the high wall, something strange happened. Instead of returning the ball, the people in the compound gave the children money to replace it. This led people to believe that those inside the compound feared the balls might contain cameras or recording devices.

FACT:

Dr. Afridi was probably never told before the raid that the person he was spying on might be Osama bin Laden.

DNA—material in cells that gives people their individual characteristics; DNA stands for deoxyribonucleic acid

vaccination—a shot of medicine that protects people from a disease

The Pakistani government was not told about the raid on the compound ahead of time. After it occurred, government officials there were furious at U.S. President Barack Obama for approving the raid in their country. They vowed to punish anyone who had helped with the raid.

Shakeel Afridi, 2010

Afridi paid a high price for his work. After the raid, the Pakistani government began rounding up anyone suspected of helping the Americans. Afridi was questioned and may have been tortured. He was sentenced to 33 years in a Pakistani prison.

U.S. officials are concerned for Afridi's safety. But relations between the United States and Pakistan have grown worse since the bin Laden raid. Many hope that in time tensions will ease and that Afridi will be released safely. But until then, he must suffer the fate of many spies—a life behind bars.

HIDING IN PLAIN SIGHT

Spies know that their activities can have deadly consequences. Some people may wonder why anyone would choose such a risky line of work. Whether they work for money or to help others, the only people who can answer that question are spies themselves. They remain hidden in plain sight, but one thing is certain. Their daring missions continue to shape the governments of our modern world.

GLOSSARY

asset (ASS-et)—an item or person of value

bug (BUG)—to place a hidden microphone

capitalism (KA-puh-tuhl-iz-uhm)—economic system that allows people to freely create businesses and own as much property as they can afford

communism (KAHM-yuh-ni-zuhm)—system in which goods and property are owned by the government and shared in common; communist rulers limit personal freedoms to achieve their goals

DNA (DEE EN AY)—material in cells that gives people their individual characteristics; DNA stands for deoxyribonucleic acid

double agent (DUH-buhl AY-juhnt)—a spy who works for one country's spy agency but is really loyal to another

embassy (EM-buh-see)—a building in one country where the representatives of another country work

extremist (ik-STREE-muhst)—a person whose views or actions are far beyond the norm

hack (HACK)—to illegally break into a computer system

handler (HAND-lur)—a person at a spy agency who serves as a contact and mentor for spies

hijack (HYE-jak)—to take illegal control of a vehicle

KGB (KAY JEE BEE)—Russian initials for the Soviet Union's Committee for State Security; the KGB was the main Soviet spy agency

mole (MOHL)—a spy who works within the government of one country while supplying secret information to another

probation (pro-BAY-shuhn)—when criminal is allowed to go free under the supervision of a probation officer

SEALs (SEELS)—a special forces group in the U.S. Navy

terrorism (TER-ur-i-zuhm)—the use of violence and destructive acts to create fear and to advance a strong set of beliefs

vaccination (vak-suh-NAY-shun)—a shot of medicine that protects people from a disease

READ MORE

Buller, Laura. *Top Secret: Shady Tales of Spies and Spying.* New York: DK Publishing, 2011.

Goodman, Michael E. *The CIA and other American Spies.* Spies Around the World. Mankato, Minn.: Creative Education, 2012.

Lunis, Natalie. *The Takedown of Osama bin Laden.* Special Ops. New York: Bearport Pub., 2012.

INTERNET SITES

FactHound offers a safe, fun way to find Internet sites related to this book. All of the sites on FactHound have been researched by our staff.

Here's all you do:

Visit *www.facthound.com*

Type in this code: 9781476501239

INDEX